# Nobody Owns A Cat

OTHER BOOKS BY NICOLE HOLLANDER
PUBLISHED BY SOURCEBOOKS:

My Cat's Not Fat, He's Just Big-Boned

Psycho Kitties

# Nobody Owns a Cat

## An Unhelpful Guide to Cat Behavior

### By Nicole Hollander

Sourcebooks Hysteria™
An Imprint of Sourcebooks, Inc.®
Naperville, Illinois

Copyright © 2000, 2007 by Nicole Hollander
Cover and internal design © 2000, 2007 by Tom Greensfelder
Sourcebooks and the colophon are registered trademarks of Sourcebooks, Inc.

All rights reserved. No part of this book may be reproduced in any form or by any electronic or mechanical means including information storage and retrieval systems—except in the case of brief quotations embodied in critical articles or reviews—without permission in writing from its publisher, Sourcebooks, Inc.

Published by Hysteria, an imprint of Sourcebooks, Inc.
P.O. Box 4410
Naperville, IL 60567-4410
(630) 961-3900
Fax: (630) 961-2168
www.sourcebooks.com

ISBN-10: 1-4022-1023-X
ISBN-13: 978-1-4022-1023-5

Printed and bound in the United States of America.
VP 10 9 8 7 6 5 4 3 2 1

## To Tom for His Friendship and Obsessive-Compulsive Design Behavior

To John and Harriet
Who Inspired This Book

# Contents

## In the Beginning

| | |
|---|---|
| Cats in Space | 13 |

## Body

| | |
|---|---|
| Give Me That Wet Food, Baby | 22 |
| Fly Me to the Moon | 27 |
| Cats Who Dress Up | 30 |
| Don't Lick That Cat | 33 |
| Oh, De Toilette | 36 |
| Slow Dancing with Your Cat | 40 |
| In the Heat of the Night | 44 |
| Vetnophobia | 49 |

## Mind

| | |
|---|---|
| Cats and the Law | 56 |
| After You're Gone | 60 |

| | |
|---|---:|
| BORED CATS | 63 |
| BRINGING HOME THE BACON | 68 |
| LIE DOWN WITH FLEAS | 72 |
| IRRITATING CATS | 79 |
| THREATENING YOUR CAT | 83 |
| FAVORITE JOKES OF CATS | 85 |
| JOKES CATS DON'T LIKE | 86 |
| LIKE TAKING CANDY FROM A BABY | 88 |
| A LETTER OF CATS | 91 |

## SPIRIT

| | |
|---|---:|
| WHILE YOU'RE UP, COULD YOU GET ME A COKE? | 96 |
| CALL ME ISHMAEL | 101 |
| THE GIRL WHO WAS RAISED BY CATS | 104 |
| CATS ARE NOT SELFISH | 109 |
| DO CATS DREAM OF COMPLIANT MICE? | 113 |
| WRITTEN IN THE STARS | 115 |
| PUSSY CATS IN HEAVEN | 130 |
| THEY HAVE WAYS OF GETTING EVEN | 133 |

# Cats in Space

## ROOTS

Why is it that the first we hear of the cat is when it appears in Egypt around 2,000 B.C. as the living embodiment of the goddess Bast? The dog was domesticated...comfortably ensconced as man's adoring servant, catching frisbees and letting his tongue loll unattractively out of his mouth, long before the cat arrived on the scene. Why? Where was the cat? Why are there no images of cats in cave paintings? Why is the Bible silent on the subject?

It's quite simple, really. Cats are not from around here. We know now that our planet was visited long ago by astronauts from a planet more intellectually advanced than ours. There is strong evidence to suggest that the planet was the Planet Hsif, and that **cats were those ancient astronauts.**

Say these cats arrive in pyramid-shaped space shuttles, they land, they reconnoiter, and someone's beeper goes off... there is an emergency at home on the Planet Hsif. Everyone drops what they are doing, the bulk of the team is hurriedly picked up by the mother ship, leaving a token force behind to gather artifacts and guard the pyramid shuttles. The main team plans to return to earth to complete their mission at the first opportunity. But their return is stymied... first by a civil war, later by budget cuts.

Those astronauts left behind await the return of their team with great patience... perhaps they stare at a spot for a year or so and then their situation hits them. They have been

abandoned. They growl, they weep, they nap, and then with the pragmatism 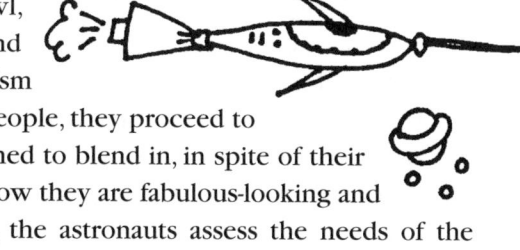 that characterizes their people, they proceed to damage control. Determined to blend in, in spite of their unusual features (they know they are fabulous-looking and this will cause jealousy), the astronauts assess the needs of the Egyptian culture and develop a coping strategy.

They will become goddesses, rat killers, and charming domestic companions all at the same time. Indispensable to Egyptian society, they are indulged and pampered, their lives protected by law. In Egypt, the punishment for killing a cat, even accidentally, was death. Families who lost their cats displayed their grief by ripping their

I DON't tHiNk tHey'LL be ABLe to LiFt HiM...tHAt WAS A JOke, MA. NO, I DON't tHiNk He's GROSS. ANy ALieN WOULD be tHRiLLeD to Get HiM.

clothes and shaving off their eyebrows. It's all been downhill since then...no wonder cats sometimes have that whiny sound in their voices.

This scenario seems to me much easier to swallow than the one history gives us: that the pyramids were built by laborers with only primitive technology and without cranes or fork lifts.

You doubt it? All cats evidence a vestigial memory of their origin. Try this experiment: bring three cats together in a room, and you will find that no matter where they are set down, they will gravitate towards each other and automatically arrange themselves into the shape of a pyramid.

There is evidence to suggest that hairballs are actually a very sophisticated means of communication and that their variety, time of day, and frequency of appearance are significant. Cats emit hairballs to signal to their people in much the same way that shipwrecked travelers build huge bonfires on the beach in hope of attracting the attention of rescue planes.

How frustrating it must be when we rush to blot out all sign of these communiques. Perhaps cats feel like prisoners who mark the days of captivity on the walls of their cells, only to have their sadistic jailers rub out the signs of their efforts as soon as they appear. I hope not. I hope they understand that we mean them no harm, that in this as in many other things, we just don't have a clue.

Some cats have made it back to Hsif. In 1988, one of our major tabloids headlined the news that hundreds of cats were disappearing, kidnapped by aliens. Au contraire, I don't think so. They haven't been kidnapped; they've been repatriated. We miss you guys, but we know you're truly happy at last.

# Give Me that Wet food, Baby
## THE MYTH OF THE DAINTY EATER

"CAN I HAVE A DONUT?"

Cats always like what you're eating better than what they're eating. They quietly move quite close to you and then very delicately reach up onto your plate and push the Sole Veronique toward themselves, while at the same time fixing you with a hypnotic stare.

Don't stare back. Don't try to distract them by getting down on all fours in front of their food and pretending it's so good you want

CAtS WHO DreAm theiR owNers' DreAms

to eat it. They aren't fooled by your performance, and you look mental down there on the floor saying, "yum, yum."

Don't let your cat force you to eat in the bedroom with the door closed, because he'll just throw his whole body against the door repeatedly until it flies open and then he'll bound onto the bed with you and your dinner, and the whole deal starts again.

When I want to eat in front of the T.V. in peace, I eat steamed asparagus. It's better for me anyway and cats don't like vegetables. Of course, I can eat anything I want, like fried chicken, and still watch television by the simple expedient of constant movement. If you keep walking and eating, your cat will soon become bored and turn to pushing tiny items off the table. Meanwhile, you're burning calories.

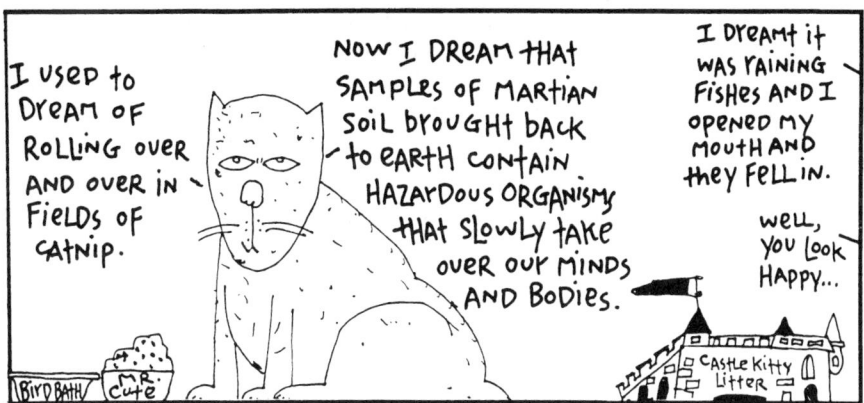

# Dear Cat Lady,

I invited a gentleman friend over for dinner the other night and you can imagine my amazement and embarrassment when my cat jumped up onto the table and made a move on my Beef Wellington garnished with rosettes of whipped potatoes—and this is not even the real embarrassing part. The real embarrassing part is that I continued to eat with one hand and used the other hand to keep the cat a safe distance away from my food and I realized this is what I do every night. I looked into the eyes of my friend and I saw that he knew it too and that he would never marry me. Has this ever happened to you?

**Dear Embarrassed in Ithaca,**
**My dear, it's happened to all of us. I know a woman who put on her false eyelashes every day of her adult life at a mirror located above the cat's dish, and it wasn't until she moved into a new apartment and put the mirror in another room that she realized that the cat would only eat if she put her false eyelashes on in front of him. She suddenly knew that she was the only woman in America who still wore false eyelashes to work, and that she hadn't been promoted in years because of it.**
**Yet, she still wears them today... why? Because her cat demands it.**

There's a rumor going around that cats, like people, must tailor their eating habits to the different stages of their lives. Kittens have different nutritional needs than adult cats. Consult with your veterinarian and then, for the good of your relationship with your cat, forget everything she tells you.

# Misconceptions About Cats

**Cats don't like sweets.**

Cats like canned food, cheap, wet, disgusting, canned food. Who can blame them? How many of us, while eating a bacon and egg sandwich on soft white bread with butter, say to ourselves, "This food is not good for me at my stage of life," and then go on blissfully stuffing those savory bites into our mouths? Why expect your cat to be more restrained than you are?

# Heartbreaking Complaints of Cats

Every Friday he brings home Cantonese food. He says I can have some if I use chopsticks. I hate him.

*tell me how you feel, don't hold back.*

## CATS IN CARS

We all know how cats feel about traveling in a car. You never see a cat with his head out the window, fur flying in the breeze. A cat is never anyone's designated driver. People infer from their hysterical behavior in cars that cats feel that way about all travel. Not true. Cats love to fly. If they had their way, they would come with you on every flight, sitting on the seat next to you, ordering a seafood dinner. When you hear of cats that have been lost in transit—their loved ones expect them in Philadelphia and they arrive, none the worse for wear, in London—don't blame the baggage handlers.

# Dear Cat Lady,

My cat doesn't like to take car rides. Is there any way I can make her more comfortable in the car?

**Dear Shirley in S.F.,**

**I can read between the lines. Basically, you're a romantic. You probably have a big-finned old Caddy convertible. You keep the top down in the coldest weather, you love your cat, and you want to share your pleasures with her... you see yourself going 110m.p.h. in that car with the cat, both of you wearing matching sunglasses and head scarves... you want your hair and her fur to look tidy when you stop at that wonderful cafe a mile up the road on the way to San Luis Obispo. I bet you carry one of those portable picnic tables in the trunk of your car just in case you see the perfect spot between the billboards... your thermos of strong coffee is always by your side... soon you plan to teach your cat to drive...**

**Grow up! In reality, the minute the engine turns over, your cat makes a noise so frightening, so bloodcurdling, that you have long since given up taking a trip of any kind with her. You can't even take her to the veterinarian for her yearly examination. Instead, you have arranged at great expense to have your vet make a house call disguised as a delivery boy, but I digress.**

**A cat can learn to tolerate car travel if you start her very young. Take your kitten for short drives every day, fill the back seat with catnip, take someone along to feed her tiny smelts.... Try to make her associate the car with fun. If you do that you may have a companion for those emergency trips to the 7-11 at midnight for non-dairy creamer, but don't count on it.**

Cats want to keep flying. They hide in the baggage compartment of the plane, with their heads turned to the wall so that the luminosity of their eyes doesn't give them away. Cats feel comfortable in the air because they originally arrived on this planet by air.

Aside from the fact that cats love to fly, there's another reason to take them along. A cat on a plane will ensure a safe trip. Have you ever heard of a plane going down with a cat on board? No, you haven't. If it's not convenient for your cat to accompany you on every flight, take something of his on board with you. A photograph or a recent rabies tag is good, but the most effective amulet is a bit of cat hair picked off the couch and placed in a silk-lined linen bag worn suspended from a silver cord around your neck.

# Cats who Dress Up

## FASHION NEEDS

Cats have a natural need to dress up. I don't care what the learned Doktor Leonard Vertu of Das Institut Für Katzen Kranken Und Schmerzen in Berlin, Germany, formerly the Prussian Pet Center, says. Dressing up in exotic outfits is as deeply rooted in cats and as natural as their admiration of fine furniture. I think his need to see something perverse in their love of costume says more about Dr. Vertu than about cats. So if your cat is a bit down in the mouth, not interested in things that formerly absorbed his attention, like licking all the emulsion off your photographs or scratching a hole in the wall-to-wall carpeting, I suggest you rummage through the bottom drawer of the dresser where you keep your costumes and start draping and bejeweling him, or better yet, take out your sewing machine and make him an outfit.

# Paper Dolls who Like for Cats to Dress up

# favorite Lamps of Cats who Dress up

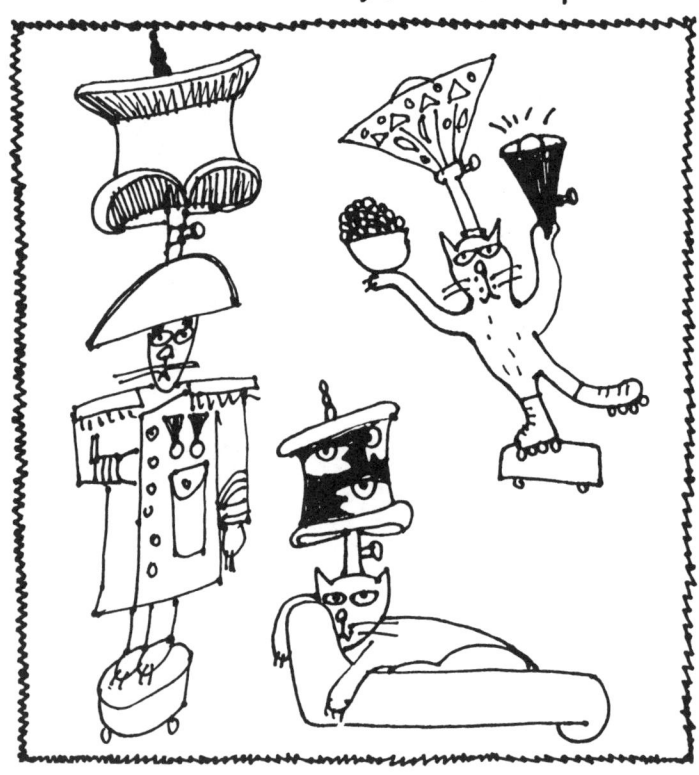

# Don't Lick that Cat

## GOOD GROOMING

Cats do groom themselves, but they tend to work on their favorite areas, letting the rest of their fur go to pot. You can help them out by grooming them with a tiny fine comb, one made of natural wood with Chinese characters embossed on it.

Grooming your cat is an activity pleasurable to both cat and owner. Your cat purrs while you hum Sinatra tunes to yourself. It's a lovely moment; don't ruin it by deciding to plait her fur into little braids all over her body and tying off the ends with tiny magenta ribbons. Don't slap your forehead and wonder out loud how he would look if you shaved his body with the exception of a star and moon-shaped fur mound on his flanks. Or it might be St. Patrick's Day and

**Dear Cat Lady,**

Last night I had a small dinner party with people I knew only slightly, and during the meal my cat sat down in the middle of the room and began to groom himself in what can only be described as an obscene fashion. My guests became visibly uncomfortable. I didn't want to call attention to his activities by removing him, so we all looked away, and the evening went downhill after that. What should I do if this happens again?

**Dear Prudish in Peoria,
Build the party around it.**

you think, "Green cat, wow!" Don't do it; the world is full of cat owners in fancy mental institutions who took that route.

Your cat's toenails should be clipped on a regular basis or her claws will grow so long that she'll sound like she's wearing high heels all the time. If your cat squirms when you clip her nails, take her to the vet to have them clipped. Your cat should always associate you with pleasure; give the vet the dirty jobs. Never, never have your cat's nails surgically removed. You'll go directly to hell if you do.

On the other hand, you might become so efficient at trimming your cat's claws that you decide to go one step further and put some purple polish on those tiny claws. Forget it, it's disgusting, paint your own nails if you must. Get a perm, buy a car, distract yourself.

# 💔 Heartbreaking Complaints of Cats

I have no interest in ripping up wall-to-wall carpeting. I'm perfectly happy to use my scratching post. Check out her fingernails... they're lethal.

*tell me how you feel, don't hold back.*

# OH, de toilette

## TOILET TRAINING YOUR CAT

Probably at one time or another you've thought of toilet training your cat or raising hermit crabs. If you've definitely decided against the crabs, read on.

I suppose you could put the litter box next to the toilet and slowly raise the box over a period of weeks, using all those *New York Times Book Review* sections you've been meaning to read or recycle or make into party hats, until the box reaches the same height as the toilet, then remove that litter box and firmly fasten a smaller litter box under the toilet seat and then after your cat gets used to balancing on the toilet seat, take the box away and loosely

stretch an old pair of panty hose under the toilet seat, putting a small amount of litter in the hose and in succeeding days make a hole in the hose and in the following days make the hole larger and larger while using less and less kitty litter until the panty hose can be removed altogether, and the cat is toilet trained... or you could just leave the cat in the bathroom with the *National Enquirer* for a few days.

Here's the hitch: cats don't flush, and they won't use a toilet that hasn't been flushed. This is not a problem unless you want to leave the house, in which case you will have to have someone else come in several times a day to flush in your stead. Most cats like to have a celebrity perform this function, like a film star or a talk show host, but if you can't get one, maybe he'll let your ex-husband do it.

If you and your cat are of opposite genders, travel presents certain problems. Do you take the cat into the washroom of your gender or his? Is it legal for a female cat to use the men's room? Is it legal everywhere but at a rock concert? Do you need separate hotel rooms? Can you become engaged to your cat?

After your cat has been toilet trained, she will want a bathroom of her own. Give it to her, she deserves it. (See Cat Bathroom/Solarium on following pages.)

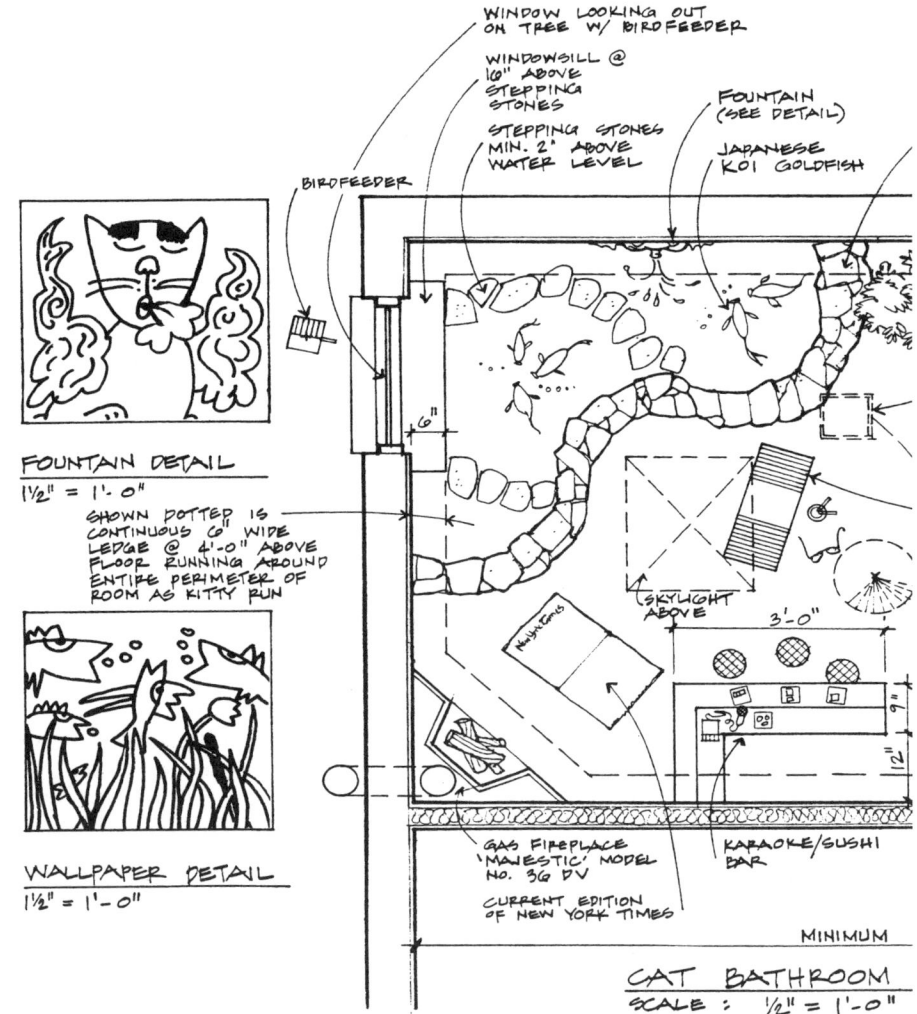

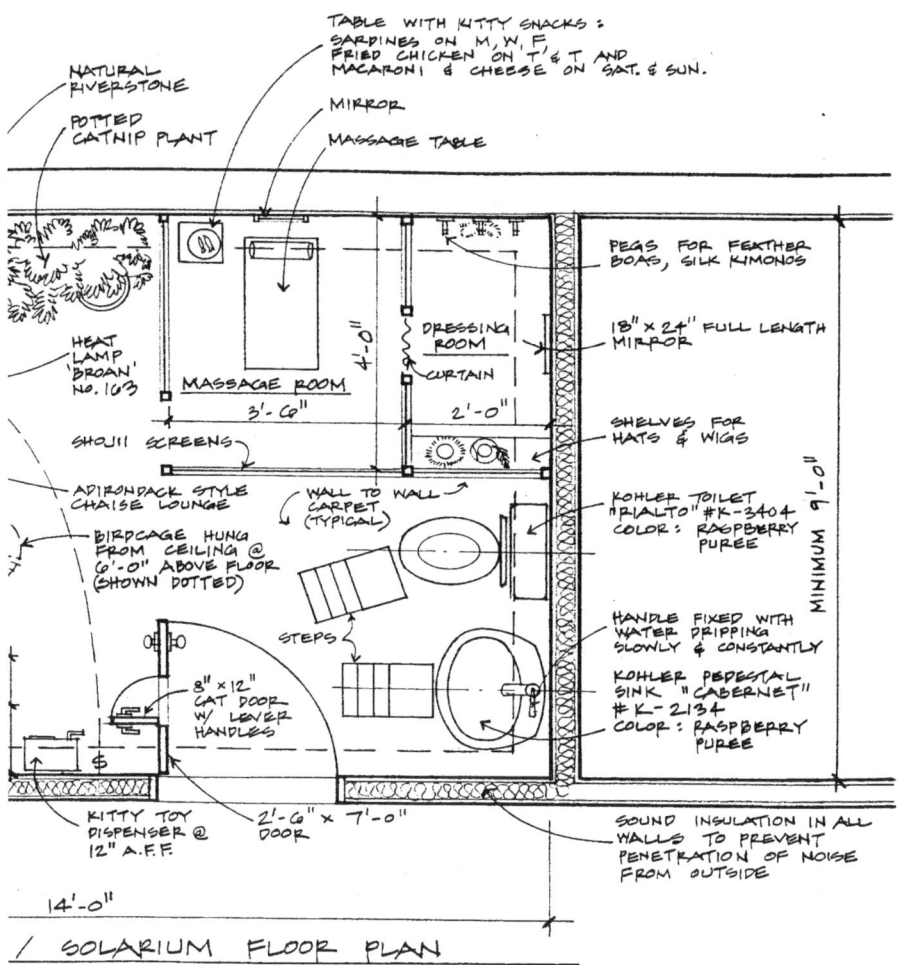

# Slow-Dancing with Your Cat

## BUILDING STRONG BODIES

When I was a little girl I heard a rumor that there were two cats in the neighborhood who swam around in a pool in their backyard. I never actually saw them. Probably cats don't like to have people watch them swim. They'd never swim at a public beach, that's not their style. I see them in my mind's eye taking a slow turn around the pool doing the breast stroke.

I once had a cat who liked to dance. I found that out by accident; they don't like you to see them doing something out of the ordinary. They figure if you see they can dance, the next thing you

# Dear Cat Lady,

I have an indoor cat and to be honest he's rather large and it's not all muscle. I don't think he's getting enough exercise. What do you think?

**Dear Worried in Wichita,**
**He's probably as big as a house and getting bigger. I don't believe that his size is due to lack of exercise.**
**I saw grease stains on your letter. You're feeding him fried chicken and donut holes, aren't you? Stop it, or get him a pair of roller blades and let him skate around the kitchen for a few minutes every morning.**

know, you'll have them learning quantum mechanics. Anyway, I was playing a Willie Nelson tune, *Georgia*, when I looked over at my cat and noticed that she had a rather dreamy look on her face. I picked her up and put her back paws on top of my feet, held her front paws in my hands and began to dance a slow two-step.

It was unbelievably awkward. I had to bend over almost in half to reach her paws. So I lifted her up and danced with her in my arms. She was not happy; cats like control. Maybe I should have let her lead. I twirled around once and she snarled. She was deeply put out. I put her down quickly and, after a moment, she began to dance alone, swaying slowly to the music.

Now we often dance away the night together. I turn the lights down low, and turn on Willie, or Ray, and we dance on separate sides of the room. She's amazingly light on her feet. Sometimes I think of buying us matching skirts that twirl, but that seems a bit over the edge.

# 💔 Heartbreaking Complaints of Cats

She plays Patsy Cline over and over. If I hear "I Fall to Pieces" one more time, I'll crack up myself. She never plays Cole Porter.

*tell me how you feel, don't hold back.*

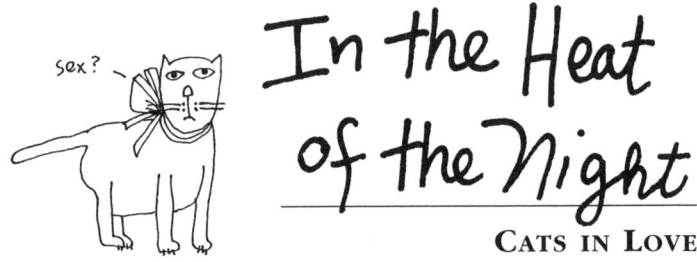

# In the Heat of the Night

## CATS IN LOVE

I recently read a description of cat sex, and I must admit it left me baffled. I can't imagine why they continue to do it, especially the female; of course, they would probably say the same of us.

Cats are a well-known asset in the early stages of romance. If you are set on having a love affair and have tired of bars and church groups, put a little harness on your cat and take her out for a walk...stop at a cafe, feed her ice cream from a silver dish.

Attractive people of both sexes will soon crowd around you and ask you out for dinner and dancing at expensive bistros. If you wish to enlarge your circle even further, place an ad in the personal section of your local newspaper: ATTRACTIVE WOMAN AND HER CAT WOULD LIKE TO MEET GOOD-LOOKING GUY FOR LONG WALKS UNDER THE STARS AND POSSIBLE TOTAL COMMITMENT.

You might argue that one of the reasons you picked a cat

Dear Cat Lady,

I know that it's irresponsible to add to the cat population when so many animals are unwanted and abandoned, but what if my cat finds out I had it neutered?

**Dear Worried in Washington,
Try to keep sexual facts away from your animals; don't let them watch T.V. Because if they do find out, they will be annoyed, and they are notoriously unforgiving.**

as a pet over a dog is that you didn't want to be out walking an animal at inconvenient times, but think of the beauty of it. You only do it when you're looking for companionship. As soon as you find a live-in mate, you can stop walking your cat and she won't mind.

# Heartbreaking Complaints of Cats

I get nervous if she comes home late, and I'd feel more comfortable if she didn't bring dates back to the apartment. On the other hand I don't want her out all night either.

tell me how you feel, don't hold back.

# Vetnophobia

## KEEPING YOUR CAT HEALTHY

The average house cat seems rather sedentary,* dividing her time between sleeping, resting her eyes, and sleeping, but around 10:00 every evening, your cat will begin to dash madly about the house—get out of her way, she's exercising. This nightly exercise, plus giving in to her every whim, should keep your cat feeling pretty darn good until she's about seventeen.

Cats, like humans, follow a familiar daily pattern, and deviation from this pattern is reason for concern. If Cousin Wilfred, who has taken his

---

*Appearances are deceiving—your cat may appear to be sleeping but really he is thinking about something you said, something that hurt him deeply or possibly he is working out a unified field theory.

# Dear Cat Lady,

My cat has a "condition," one of those which, while not serious, is incurable. This condition causes his nose to run constantly; in addition he makes an awful sniffling sound. I've tried wearing ear plugs, but that didn't work—I could still hear him. So I wore a pair of ear muffs over the ear plugs, and then I couldn't hear the phone. I'm thinking of giving him away, what do you think?

**Dear Insensitive and Not Deserving to Have a Cat at All in Cincinnati,**

**Relationships are difficult. No doubt there are things you do that your cat finds objectionable. Perhaps he hates your perfume—I bet you use Giorgio—but he doesn't carry on, does he? No, he pretends not to notice. On the other hand, he could be carrying a grudge, just biding his time, until cats take over the world and he exiles you to the Dry Tortugas.**

**But that's all the more reason to be nice to him while you still have the upper hand... we'll need all the goodwill we can muster when the main team of cat astronauts returns to Earth from the Planet Hsif (see CATS IN SPACE), forcing most of us into serfdom, manning catfish farms and cooking fried chicken day and night for their insatiable appetites. You get the picture.**

seat in front of the television at 7:00 every evening for twenty years, consuming exactly one six pack of beer and a large combination Tombstone pizza before retiring at 10:35, were suddenly to order the Mongolian Beef with pea pods, there would be cause for alarm. If your cat loses his appetite or takes up residence in the closet, call your vet immediately. Cats hate to go to the vet,** so if your cat seems under the weather, have the vet come to your home.

You might wonder how you can afford to pay a vet to come to your home. Cat insurance should be available everywhere soon. We can only hope that cat insurance will not be as big a rip-off as our own health insurance. I am personally opposed to health insurance; I believe that the chance of being covered for a really serious illness is about as likely as winning big at the craps table in Vegas. Be sure to read your cat's policy carefully to make sure that you are covered for loss of income if your cat is unable to perform his regular work.

---

\*\* There are cats so starved for attention that they will pretend to be ill just to get noticed. Male cats will often feign pregnancy in order to see that incredulous look spread across your face as you reach for the phone to contact a tabloid newspaper. False pregnancy is a call for help. Luckily there are cat therapists who specialize in Feline Malingering. Look under Family Therapists in the yellow pages, and be prepared to stay in there for the long haul. Problems of feline self-esteem often involve every member of the family with countless sessions and huge bills.

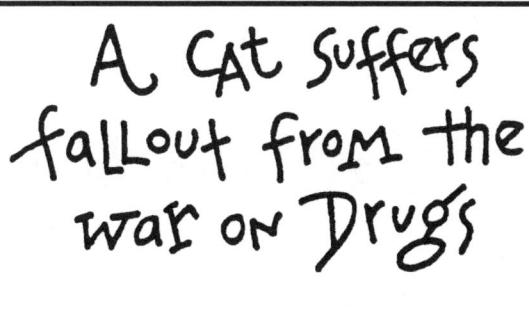

# Cats and the Law

## LEGAL RIGHTS OF CATS

The following list of laws governing our behavior toward cats is by no means complete. The full list is contained in a two-volume leather-bound set, and is available upon written request from your local CLAW (Cat Law) office or by calling 1-800-CLAW.

Cats carry more political clout than you think, considering that only one of our Presidents was a cat owner while in the White House. (Of course, we don't know how many of our Commanders-in-Chief

walked a dog in public and kept a cat in private.) A low public profile seems to suit the feline temperament. Cats work most effectively behind the scenes... their lobby is rumored to be both well-funded and discreet.

Some of the laws governing behavior toward cats carry rather heavy penalties, so read the list carefully. If you're considering a move from one jurisdiction to another, contact your local office of CLAW for a listing of the legal rights of cats in your area.

## STATUTES

• In California, if you leave a cat alone in a car that is neither a convertible nor a BMW, you may be liable for a heavy fine, and fifty-two weeks of public service.

• In Florida, a cat who is dressed in a costume not of his choosing can sue for humiliation benefits. Some-times these damage awards are in the six figures.

• In New York, a cat who is subjected to musical tastes not his own may ask that the offender's stereo be seized.

• In every state but North

Carolina, a cat's right to be out at night is acknowledged. In addition, the law recognizes the danger to a cat who is out alone at night and requires that the cat's owner follow him at a discreet distance to protect him from harm.

- In New Orleans, Louisiana, it is unlawful to feed a cat red beans and rice for breakfast, even if he begs. Cats may eat only a beignet and milky coffee before noon.

- In Santa Fe, a fine of $1,000 may be levied on someone who entertains the thought out loud of having a cat declawed. Actual declawing of a cat is a capital offense in every state, although no one has been drawn and quartered for this offense in over ten years.

# Heartbreaking Complaints of Cats

If she sees a cat on the street, she has to bring it home... Some of them were probably just out for a breath of fresh air. It's pathological, we have seven cats now. Only crazy people have an odd number of cats.

Tell me how you feel, don't hold back.

FINANCIAL PLANNING CAN'T be over-emphasized.

# After You're Gone
## Providing for Your Cat in Your Will

What if, while you're on vacation having a good time and your cat is at home sleeping off her depression, you decide to go bungee jumping and you have a fatal accident? Is your cat provided for? Have you discussed your cat's future with family, with friends? Have you appointed a guardian for your cat? Who will take care of your cat if you're disabled or dead? Your sister?

Does your sister feel the same way about your cat as you do, or would she as soon push that cat off a moving train as look at her? Do you think your sister has ever forgiven you for that little incident in the summer of '62?

Over one million dog owners have provided for their pets in their wills. What have you done for your cat? Before you go running off to your lawyer in a fit of remorse, take a moment to think it over.

# Cat Quizzes

*What percentage of pet owners keeps a photograph of their pets in their wallets?*

**1. 40% of pet owners keeps a photograph of their pets in their wallets.**

**2. Everyone except one man in Cincinnati keeps a photograph of their pets in their wallets.**

Perhaps there's a reason why more dogs are named beneficiaries in wills than cats. Maybe it's because dogs are feeble creatures with low self-esteem, unable to fend for themselves. Maybe a cat would prefer to learn a trade and be self-sufficient after you're gone.

Actually, I doubt that. I think your cat would prefer to be waited on hand and foot and live in the lap of luxury as long as it's presented to her as if she's doing you the favor by taking the ranch in Arizona off your hands or as if you owe her one for saving you from drowning in a previous life.

BORED BEYOND BELIEF.

# Bored Cats

## AMUSING THE CITY CAT

I knew a cat once who begged to be taken on a trip with his owners. He suggested by means of sign language and his ability to let a single tear fall and remain suspended on his cheek that he was bored and had been robbed of his birthright by spending so much time confined to a city apartment. He needed to be in

Misconceptions About Cats

**Cats don't use mail order catalogs.**

CATS WHO EDUCATE THEMSELVES.

I TAUGHT MYSELF TO READ AND THEN I SENT AWAY FOR CATALOGS.

AND THEN I ORDERED 50 POUNDS OF SMOKED SALMON FROM HARRY AND DAVID.

I COULDN'T OPEN THE MAILBOX, IT WAS CRAMMED WITH CATALOGS... WHAT'S THAT SMELL?

nature to feel whole. He needed to feel the sun on his fur, the breeze on his nose, to climb tall trees and to hear the songs of birds close-up.

The gullible young couple fell for his performance and took him on that trip. They packed games and food and drink and toys and prepared to enjoy themselves... we need not dwell on the car trip. Suffice it to say the cat refused to stay in his carrier, and as soon as the couple started singing, "A Hundred Bottles of Beer on the Wall," he slid under the driver's seat and pressed the gas pedal, causing the driver to lose control and crash into the car in

I'm afraid my cat may be bored while I'm at work. Should I get her one of those cat videos?

**Dear Worried in Washington,
A number of videos for cats are on the market. They are full of birds and fish, moving about provocatively. I don't think cats care for them. I think cats would rather see films of people taking pratfalls.**

front of him. No more than twenty cars were involved in the accident and no one was hurt. After leaving the sheriff's office, the couple decided to continue the trip. Reaching the nature preserve, the three ran from the car to experience nature during the few minutes left in the day. A leaf dropped from a tree onto the cat, terrifying him. He fell into a coma, coming to only hours later in his apartment as he was being combed and spoon-fed chicken nuggets. He has never been taken on a family trip again and resents it deeply.

# Heartbreaking Complaints of Cats

OKAY, I DID HAVE A MASSAGE LAST WEEK, AND I DID CHARGE IT TO HIS ACCOUNT. I CARRY A LOT OF TENSION IN MY NECK. HE KNOWS THAT. He's TERRIBLY CHEAP.

TELL ME HOW YOU FEEL, DON'T HOLD BACK.

# Bringing Home the Bacon

## CATS WHO WORK

Cats have been productive members of society throughout history, but until recently their jobs have been restricted to rodent control or to keeping down the bird population. This is fine for most cats, but in every generation there are those felines who chafe

## Dear Cat Lady,

Sometimes I wonder, if I really was willing to devote time to developing my cat's potential, what could she be capable of? What if I quit my job and spent all day with her, teaching her to read, or to carry a simple tune? What if the the only books I exposed her to were computer manuals? I'd have to get rid of all my novels and my compact disc player and my three T.V.s so as not to distract her and then maybe she'd teach herself to use the computer.

Do you think she could write a series of bestselling books or would her imagination be atrophied by lack of exposure to literature or the wider world? Not that her books would have to be blockbusters, or even particularly interesting, but surely the first book written by a cat should have some sales potential...but if it did sell I'd probably have to do talk shows...I'm not going on *David Letterman*, he makes me nervous...so if I devoted this quality time to her, could she eventually earn enough to support me? Could we move to a warmer place? Am I being selfish? Perhaps my cat would be happier in a service job?

**Dear Fred in Fresno,**
**Get a life.**

under their limited opportunities and long to leave their mark. They may even become neurotic if they are thwarted. Some frustrated cats rub their foreheads against every object and person in a room; this is the behavior of a cat who has repeatedly come up against the glass ceiling.

Cats who spray have reached the end of their rope, and you just want to get out of their way or let them have their own apartment. So before you find yourself with a cat whose anti-social behavior prevents you from ever having guests, encourage your cat to express himself positively.

Don't try to direct his goals. Lots of people are frustrated nuclear physicists and want to live through their cats, or fantasize that their cats will support them in their old age. These people shouldn't have cats, they should have children. If you want what's best for your cat, just leave him plenty of fresh felt-tip markers and unlined paper. Cats hate paper with lines.

# Heartbreaking Complaints of Cats

She said I jumped up and down on the remote control, changing the channel 50 times in a minute. It wasn't me, it was her hyperactive boyfriend.

tell me how you feel, don't hold back.

# Lie Down with Fleas

## CATS WHO HATE THE DOGS WHO LOVE THEM

Cats ran wild and free with the wind in their hair searching out small dinosaurs for dinner long after the dog had become man's best friend, which accounts for the somewhat contemptuous attitude cats have toward the canine species. Dogs are joiners; if they were guys, their idea of a good time would be to attend an Elks luncheon,

have a little cottage cheese with catsup, and listen to their insurance agent lecture on fostering the entrepreneurial spirit in young boys.

Cats, on the other hand, would probably like to spend the noon hour in an elegant penthouse apartment eating fried shrimp and dropping water bombs on unsuspecting pedestrians. Dogs are good-hearted creatures, basically Libras, wanting everyone to be happy. A mature dog might even adopt an orphaned litter of cats, might even carry the kittens around in her mouth. Those kittens might even learn to say woof, woof if they need to, but they'd be biting their lips the whole time.

Most of us are animal lovers. We insist that we love all animals equally—the hamster, the weasel, and the zebra—but if pressed, we will admit to being either a cat person or a dog person.

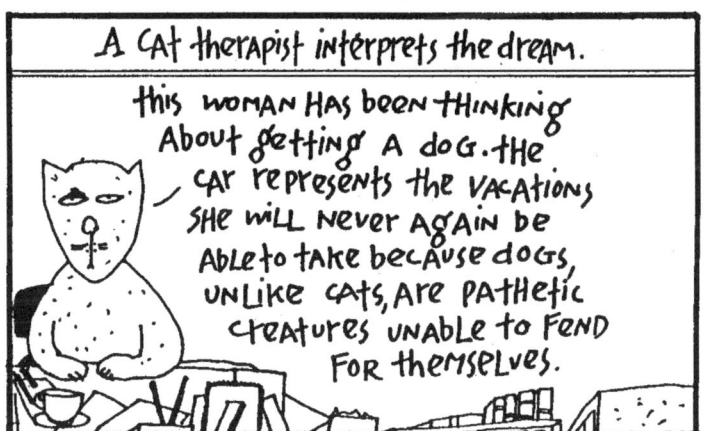

# Cat Quizzes

*Do cats and dogs have a common lineage?*

**1. Yes, the miacid, a civet-like animal that lived sixty million years ago, was the ancestor of both the cat family (Felidae) and the dog family, Canidae.**

**2. No, cats and dogs might as well be from different planets. They have nothing, nothing in common.**

People who must have both a dog and a cat are the kind of people who need balance at any cost. They are the folks who keep trying to have a girl so that their family can achieve gender symmetry and then they wake up one morning and notice that they have seven boys and wonder how it happened. If you're one of those, bring your cat and dog together when they are very young and then lie to one of them about his species.

# Heartbreaking Complaints of Cats

I hate the way dogs pant, especially in the summer. Their tongues are always hanging out... not an attractive sight. I say keep 'em at home, let them use a litter box.

tell me how you feel, don't hold back.

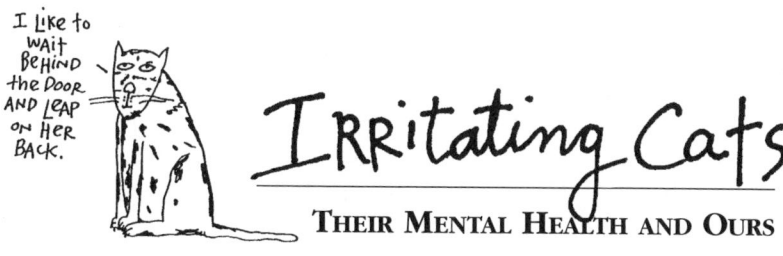

# Irritating Cats
## THEIR MENTAL HEALTH AND OURS

It seems one can't pick up a magazine or newspaper without reading that owning a cat has therapeutic value. Petting a cat lowers the blood pressure, whereas relating to people raises it... I believe that, just as I believe that red wine flushes cholesterol from your arteries and that the fat in foie gras is closer to olive oil in its molecular makeup than lard and pretty darn good for you.

But is watching public television and petting a purring cat reason enough to live? What if we need to have our blood

# Cat Quizzes

*So you think you have us figured out?*

*You wake up one morning and when you look in the mirror you notice you have makeup on or perhaps you are wearing a party hat. What's going on?*

**1. You had too much to drink the night before and forgot to remove your makeup or your party hat before retiring. This happens to all of us occasionally and there is no cause for alarm. If it happens more than once a week, go to your video store and rent *Lost Weekend* starring Ray Milland. View it five or six times. This should prevent a recurrence.**

**2. While you were asleep your cats made you up and then took pictures of their handiwork. Check the back of the top drawer of your dresser under your socks and you'll find photographs of yourself that are unappealing to say the least. Don't bother destroying them; the cat has the negatives.**

pressure raised once a day and there's no family member around to do it? Perhaps one is recently divorced or our teenage child has left for boarding school and we are bored to tears.

What if, driven by our boredom, we consider taking up field hockey or picking up men in bars with Kennedy in their surname? The last thing we need is a passive pet, purring and looking at us adoringly. It mocks our whole life experience.

Give me a cat who sits on my lap purring one minute and ripping into my flesh the next. Give me a cat who knocks down knick-knacks and large appliances unless you feed him live lobster. Give me a cat who likes to puke on an 18th-century

rug. My advice is to live with a cat so menacing that he carries his own liability insurance.

# 💔 Heartbreaking Complaints of Cats

I'm very sensitive to noise, especially the vacuum cleaner. If she cared about me, she'd use a broom, am I right?

Tell me how you feel, don't hold back.

## MODIFYING CAT BEHAVIOR

Does your cat exhibit behavior that you find vexing, perhaps maddening? Does he get up very early on weekends, leap to the top of the built-in bookcase in your headboard and drop paperbacks onto you until you get up and fix his breakfast? Does he eat messily, flinging his dry food around the kitchen? Does he sit on your newspaper when you're trying to finish a story about Oprah or Fergie?

Your cat is your spiritual guide. She is with you in this life to teach. Perhaps this time around it's lessons in patience, or tolerance, or resignation, or even total surrender. Some owners of cats are unable to learn from their cats and try to change the cat's

behavior. They threaten them, they tell them horrifying tales of disobedient cats who came to a bad end. These people often show up in the next life as water beetles or politicians.

# Favorite Jokes of Cats

"Quite amusing."

In a survey of 182,000,000 cats, we found that these were the cartoons most cats found amusing.

# Jokes Cats don't Like

In a survey of the same 182,000,000 cats they chose these cartoons as hurtful, but not necessarily untrue.

# Like taking Candy from a Baby

## CATS WHO PLAY MIND GAMES WITH THEIR OWNERS

I don't like to give my cat the opportunity to make a fool of me. If things are slightly out of order when I get home—the door to the medicine cabinet is ajar, the top drawer of my bureau is open a crack—I pretend not to notice. I don't want them laughing behind my back. I don't ask them for small favors. I don't say: "While you're up could you turn off that light, it's shining in my eyes?" I get up and do it myself. I don't talk to them about my day, I don't ask for their advice: "Do you think this dress looks better on me than the blue one? Should I buy an American car?"

# Dear Cat Lady,

My cat has been in the basement for weeks. Every evening, I put food at the top of the stairs; it remains untouched, but the dog has disappeared. Last night, I stood at the top of the stairs and called, "Hey kitty, kitty," but he didn't respond. I thought I heard music and then someone said, "Come on down, little honey."

The next day I took the rope off the swing set, a serrated knife from the silverware drawer, two flashlights—one for heft and the other one for its narrow beam of light—and a nine iron from my father's old golf bag. I heated some water on the stove, I put it in a big thermos, and for good measure I twisted up a long cone of newspaper and lit it.

I opened the door to the basement. I said, "Here kitty, kitty," but no one answered. I carried the torch and the thermos and the nine iron and the flashlights and the serrated knife with me and I ran pell-mell down the narrow stairs into the waiting darkness. I smelled an acrid smell; the smell brought tears to my eyes. Perhaps it's a gas leak or perhaps the odor of hundreds of cats massed shoulder to shoulder at the base of the stairs, their tiny mouths open, sharp teeth glistening... breathing heavily. I turned around and ran back up the stairs. What do you suggest?

**Dear Creeped Out in Crescent City,**
**Brick up the basement.**

You're just asking for trouble if you do that. They lose respect for you; they don't even try to hide it—they're openly smirking at you—they don't even bother to turn away and pretend to wash themselves.

Pretty soon other cats on the street look at you funny. I don't know how one cat communicates your vulnerability to the other cats. I don't think they can use the phone, but how would I know? I live here at their sufferance. They could turn me out at any time if they knew how to use the can opener, which they don't. Ha!

# A Letter of Cats
## SAVING THE POSTAL SYSTEM

An Open Letter to the U.S. Postmaster General:

Recently, you conducted a national survey to choose between two Elvis stamps. Okay, Elvis was cool, but cats are even more popular than Elvis. I remember when the Beatles got in trouble when they said they were more popular than Jesus. Well, I'm not saying that. I'm just saying cats are the nation's number-one pet.

If you people at the Post Office ever want to get out of the deep financial hole you're in, put out a series of cat stamps. People will snap them up, people who haven't written a letter in years—what am I saying? All your stamps could have cats on them.

You could have Christmas cats, Passover cats, cats in space...the mind boggles. Famous artists and photographers would offer their services pro bono. Forget piddling incremental rises in the price of

stamps. You could charge anything you want for these babies.

With the increased revenue flowing into agency coffers, the Post Office could be self-supporting in a year. In three years, the Postal Service could reinstitute twice-daily mail delivery.

Other nations would envy us. Post Offices could be architectural gems, centers of art, theater and dance. Wages could be increased; working conditions would be pleasant and safe. There would be no disgruntled employees with automatic weapons roaming about; uniforms would be designed by Ralph Lauren and Isaac Mizrahi. People would vie to work in the Postal Service. When you appeared at their window, they would smile at you and speak in poetry. Yes, it can be done!

# While you're up, Could you get me a Coke?

## COMMUNICATING WITH CATS

I love a well-made bed, the sheets so taut you could bounce a penny off them. My sheets and comforter match. Of course I iron the sheets, and they smell delicious, not of roses or lavender, but of a scent I have made specially for me, Basil and Lemon. I wear a freshly laundered l00% cotton nightgown, simply embroidered by a woman in Switzerland, an old friend of my mother's. I pull back

## Dear Cat Lady,

I fully understand that if you ask a cat a question like: "What two states have the longest contiguous border?" he won't answer. A cat may not feel like answering or he may not know the answer. I accept that. On the other hand, my cat will not even help in an emergency. I accidentally let the water overflow in the tub and there was water all over the floor. I shouted for him to bring some paper towels. Nothing, nada, I could have been talking to myself. What is it with cats?

**Dear Righteously Angry But Off-Base,**
**I can understand that when faced with a flooded bathroom floor, you lost control and made a direct request of your cat. They don't like that. If you had waited a bit longer before getting hysterical, he would have brought you one of those fluffy beach towels and helped you mop up, perhaps even fixed you a hot toddy, but you'll never know, will you?**

the comforter and slide between the sheets, which are delightfully cool; I turn off my bedside lamp and lie on my back, hands limp at my sides, and look out at the night sky... I feel the soft breeze from the window, just open a crack... so perfect... sleep is one of the last great safe sensual experiences left to us today, don't you agree? My white cat, Edgar, is curled up at my feet; he also matches the comforter and the sheets. I fold my hands across my chest and savor the moment just before I drift into sleep.

Oh, hell! The light in the hallway is on; it's shining in my eyes. I can't sleep with the light on. I look into my cat Edgar's large kind face, and I say, "Please turn off the hallway light," and he looks at me for a long while, then quite deliberately squeezes his eyes shut. I never ask him to do anything twice. It's demeaning. I should know better by now. All my questions to Edgar are by definition rhetorical, but he has other fine qualities. I'm sure.

# Heartbreaking Complaints of Cats

He comes home every day and complains about his job. It's a constant bummer. I'd like to hear a little good news for a change.

Tell me how you feel, don't hold back.

They named me "Sex Machine." You know, after the James Brown song. Sort of a joke at my expense, right? So when I have to go to the vet and she asks my name, they lose their nerve... they tell her: "Frisky." It isn't enough I have to go to the vet, I have to have an identity crisis too? I could spit.

# Call Me Ishmael

## NAMING YOUR CAT

Kittens are so adorable that you may find yourself talking baby talk to them.

Okay, you'll get over it. More dangerous than that is giving them a name that you'll be ashamed to tell others. I have a friend who named her cat Debutante, but she never told anyone. I

# Dear Cat Lady,

I just acquired my first kitten and I'm trying to decide what to name her. I know that this name is one we will both have to live with forever, because you can't just keep changing an animal's name or they get very neurotic, just as you or I would if someone kept changing our names, so my point is that I have to be very careful here.

First I plan to buy several of those books that list names and their meanings. I realize these are books for naming babies and they may not apply in the case of cats, but it's a start. Then I have to decide whether I want to name her after one of the goddess cults that are cat-identified or whether I should name her for a woman in history I admire, or give her a kind of normal person name, or give her an androgynous name, or a name associated with her breed's country of origin or her coloring.

I read about a government economist who named and renamed his dog after the person who was annoying him most at any given moment, so that he could shout at the dog, "Sit, John Kenneth Galbraith, sit, roll over, stay, play dead, fetch." I think this is disrespectful. I would never do that to an animal. What I'm trying to say is, it's a big decision and I'd appreciate your input.

**Dear Highly Neurotic in Newark,**
**I had to take a number of Quaaludes after reading your letter. Just name the cat Sally.**

never knew her cat had a name. The cat was always referred to as "she."

Before you decide on a name for your cat, imagine yourself in a room full of friends. Perhaps you've had a drink or two and you're just relaxed enough to let your cat's silly name slip out. There is a short silence and then your friends, never tactful at the best of times, giggle at you. And what's worse is you know they feel they have a deep insight into your character and whatever dignity you had is out the window.

# the Girl Who was Raised by Cats

**A Furry Tale**

Mary Beth wandered off in Bloomingdale's and was raised in the wild by cats. They renamed her Audrey and taught her many things.

When the cats had taught her everything they could, they sent her off to Harvard University.

Audrey fits in quite well at Harvard except for an occasional lapse...

When she calls pet shops to see how many birds they have in stock.

> Some friends introduce her to Roger Byrd the III. His name stirs her feline instincts, which she mistakes for love.

> Audrey and her mother are reunited. They plan the wedding.

## As the wedding approaches, Audrey wonders...

Should I tell Roger about my past? What if he finds out the truth by himself?

Oh, what the heck, why fix it if it ain't broke?

As Audrey walks down the aisle to the strains of "Feelings" (which she secretly thinks of as "Felines"),

the guests' eyes mist over with tears... which is lucky because when Audrey stops to scratch at a pew and hiss at her in-laws, practically no one notices. The happy couple are united and should live happily ever after, unless Audrey's past comes back to haunt them.

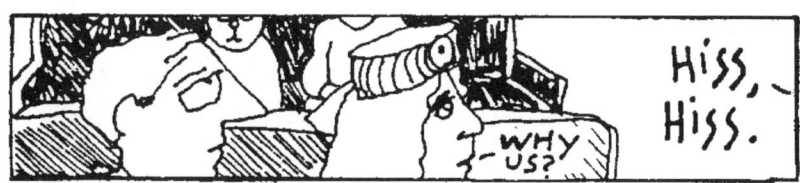

# Cats Are Not Selfish

## INTERPRETING AMBIGUOUS BEHAVIOR

I read about a poet who built a new house identical to his old one so his cat would not be disoriented by unfamiliar surroundings. I understand that. I've been wearing the same black sweater and sweat pants for years, because those are the clothes my cat prefers.

When I worked in an office, I would leave the house in that outfit and then change in the nearest phone booth, back when we

still had phone booths. When the phone company saw fit to put pay phones out in the open over those little shelves, I was forced to work at home. Working at home has some advantages...when my black outfit is in the wash, I can work in my underwear. Yes, my underwear is also black.

I don't want to leave the impression that my cat is not grateful or that cats in general are takers. There are cats who always have the welfare of those they live with uppermost in their minds.

I knew a cat who stood in front of the television, only when his owners had the set on. Reginald, the cat, stood his ground against

Dear Cat Lady,

My cat turns off my answering machine while I'm at work. As a result, I don't return important calls. My friends feel I'm ignoring them and have stopped calling. My cat is ruining my social life. What can I do?

**Dear Lonely in Laredo,**
**Pleeze, I hate it when people blame their lack of a social life on their cats. Like all cats, your cat lives only to make you happy. In this case, he is protecting you from the knowledge that no one ever calls you. He doesn't want you to realize the full extent of your unpopularity, so he turns off the machine. Be grateful, you cad.**

a barrage of insults from his loved ones...let's call them Ruth and Dennis. They insisted that he move away from the set, that he was blocking their view, that he thought of himself as invisible when in fact he was a large, overweight cat and more.

That cat stood his ground solely because he felt that Ruth and Dennis watched too much television. He was hoping that he could make television-watching such a chore that they would turn off the set and read a book. That cat lived in hope, and died disappointed.

# Heartbreaking Complaints of Cats

I'm so lonely. they never invite other cats over to visit me. I'm not unfriendly. I'd gladly share my toys and food with a strange cat. He could sit in my favorite chair, really.

tell me how you feel, don't hold back.

# Do Cats Dream of Compliant Mice?

## Dream Analysis

Statistics tell us that cats spend 65% of their time sleeping. Sometimes they moan in their sleep, their tails twitch, their bodies jerk. They are dreaming, but of what?

*I WASN'T SLEEPING*

Do they dream of frenetic sex at Mardi Gras? Or perhaps they dream of the hunt, the thrill of the chase across the veldt, the conquest of wild creatures under a brilliant blue sky; or do they dream an urban dream of a cramped apartment filled with hyperkinetic, suicidal mice, piling their bodies at the feet of a beaming master?

*I WAS THINKING ABOUT SOMETHING YOU SAID...*

Perhaps they fantasize meeting a wealthy older couple, catless, who, after looking around their elegant living

113

room in the south of France with its pale carpeting, white couches and collection of Tiffany glass, realize how pathetic and empty their lives are without a pet and beg him to come and live with them. Or perhaps they dream of revenge...

*there's a lot of Scorpio in my chart.*

# Written in the Stars

## Astrological Cats

Cats were held in high esteem in early Chinese and Japanese cultures, not only because of their expertise in rat-catching, but because of the meditative aspect of their natures... you know that look they get when they are staring at a speck of dust?

Legend has it that a cat attended the funeral of Buddha, but marred the solemnity of the occasion by licking himself obscenely while humming show tunes. As a result of his momentary loss of decorum, the cat was omitted from the Chinese and Japanese zodiacs. And in retaliation for that slur, no cat has eaten Chinese or Japanese food from that day to this.

*Some of us have relented and do have the occasional sushi.*

In our Western astrological system, which is a symbolic one, the cat is represented by Leo. That couldn't be more appropriate. There's not a cat alive who's not part Leo, born to be the center

# Dear Cat Lady,

I have fallen in love with a man who has a cat. I've never cottoned to cats, but I'm prepared to adore this one... So far, he doesn't seem prepared to adore me. What can I do to change that? Money is no object.

**Dear Born to Be Taken Advantage Of, Find out the cat's birthday and buy him a present appropriate to his astrological sign. (See following guide). If that doesn't do the trick, feed him little bits of fried chicken whenever you visit, and if that doesn't work, look for a new boyfriend.**

of attention, the focus of every group. But, of course, each cat has his individual birth sign.

Consider his sign carefully before buying him gifts or making any changes in your life that involve packing up your belongings in cardboard boxes. In addition, you would be well-advised to have an astrological compatibility chart drawn up for the two of you, plus one for anyone you are considering a long-term relationship with. It is only by consulting his chart that you can understand your cat fully and learn to modify your behavior accordingly.

# the Aquarius Cat

### January 20 to February 18

the aquarian cat is the most independent of cats. He/she may flirt with you and then move on, but once a commitment is made, this cat is yours for life. Place an orchid in their water dish, but don't try to change their minds. If you're going to a concert in Salzberg, take this cat along.

# the Pisces Cat
## February 19 to March 20

the Pisces cat is the most emotional of cats. they often write poems to their owners. full of enthusiasm, capable of self-deception, often late, they do best with a calm, steady companion. take them to lunch under a willow tree, preferably in Seville.

# the Aries Cat

### MARCH 21 to APRIL 19

the Aries cat falls in love easily, one minute purring in your lap, the next running off with an interesting stranger. Charming, enthusiastic, energetic, but lacks patience. Buy the Aries cat a diamond collar and take him/her to Italy.

# the taurus cat

### April 20 to May 20

Serve your Taurus cat the same meal every day... as long as it's lobster. Appeal to this cat's sensual side, (massage is good) and they're yours forever. Taurus cats are great gift-givers and often leave surprises around the house for their owners.

# the Gemini Cat
## MAY 21 to JUNE 20

AH! the Gemini Cat, so intellectual, original, verbal, and witty (can do Groucho Marx at the drop of a hat). But beware. This cat is easily bored. Keep them amused with toys or games or they may get edgy and start looking for a new home.

# The Cancer Cat

### June 21 to July 22

The Cancer Cat is the most maternal of cats. They often chase after their owners to make sure they've eaten properly, and they like to fluff your pillows. Watch out, they hold a grudge. Tell them you're sorry and take them to Europe to buy antiques.

# the Leo Cat
## July 23 to August 22

Leo cats rarely speak, as sounds are not necessary to ensure their dominance over everyone. Should they open their mouths, you would see their preference for gold inlays.
Their color is hot pink. They tend to be large.

# the Virgo Cat

### August 23 to September 22

The Virgo cat is meticulous and critical. Keep their litter box clean or they'll get even. They are the only cats with their own toothpaste. They love flowers, natural fabrics, and the color beige.

# the Libra Cat
## September 23 to October 22

the Libra cat likes to be out socializing. this cat likes group activities, wants everybody to be happy, needs its fur combed a lot, likes lizards, pale green, and the city of Antwerp.

# the Scorpio Cat

## october 23 to November 21

The Scorpio Cat wants your full attention. He/she had better be an "only" child. Emotionally intense, these cats look terrific against a blood red or burgundy background. Their intricate, power-hungry natures often lead them to settle in Paraguay or Washington, D. C.

# The Sagittarian Cat

## November 22 to December 21

The Sagittarian Cat is one of the most entertaining of cats. Romantic, restless, and charming, they enhance any gathering. Buy them an elegant watch, but don't expect them to be on time.

# The Capricorn Cat

### December 22 to January 19

The Capricorn Cat is serious and ambitious when young, but wonderfully mellow when mature. Beware of the cat's dry sense of humor, often expressed by jumping into the laps of people with allergies.

# 💔 Heartbreaking Complaints of Cats

He accused me of drinking all the water from the Christmas tree stand. It wasn't me... I think it was reindeer.

*Tell me how you feel, don't hold back.*

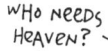

# Pussy Cats in Heaven

### A Song for Three Cats

There won't be no pussy cats in heaven,
No tabbies in them abbies in the skies,
Your feline'll make a beeline for the other place you see,
'Cause pussy cats will only tell you lies.

No, you will find you just can't trust your kitty,
To ask your cat the facts would be unwise,

They're lyin', alibiin', falsifyin' you and me,
'Cause a pussy cat will only tell you lies.

Oh, you may find a hamster in Valhalla,
A trusty dog or hog or frog in paradise,
But there won't be no pussy cats in heaven,
'Cause a pussy cat will only tell you lies.

Oh, you can trust a chicken with a secret,
And a ferret'll fairly rarely verbalize,
But a kitty will not pity confidentiality,
'Cause a pussy cat will only tell you lies.

—From the musical SYLVIA'S REAL GOOD ADVICE

# Heartbreaking Complaints of Cats

Just because there's goose down all over their bedroom, they accuse me of ripping a hole in the comforter. Why me? Maybe geese got into the boudoir.

*tell me how you feel, don't hold back.*

# they have Ways of Getting Even
## KEEPING YOUR CAT HAPPY

Your cat's mental health is in your hands. Far from being the remote creatures of the dog lover's imagination, cats are highly emotional animals. They respond to your every mood. If you are happy, they are happy; if you are depressed, they are depressed, and they hate it. If you are down in the mouth for too long, say more than twenty-four hours, if you cry for no reason, if you stay in your bathrobe for

the entire weekend, your cat will suffer. He may develop fleas even though he's an indoor cat, or begin nipping your ankles and licking the life out of your plants. Remember this behavior is not his fault, it's yours. A cat is easy to please, but sensitive to atmosphere, so provide him with the environment that brings out the best in him.

I know you think you have enough to put up with, given the state of the economy and coming to terms with the knowledge

**Dear Cat Lady,**

I was raised to believe that when I died I would arrive at the pearly gates to be greeted by a white Anglo-Saxon American angel who would look in his record book and ask me a few easy questions and welcome me to a charming place with good music, but last night I dreamt that cats were in charge of heaven. It was quite a disturbing idea. Would my behavior toward my cat stand up to the scrutiny of a cat with wings and a halo?

**Dear Stricken by a Guilty Conscience in Syracuse,**
**You've done something you're ashamed of, haven't you? You can't quite bring yourself to write it down, but I know. Perhaps you recently gave your cat a pill or maybe you locked the door to the bedroom so that he is no longer free to sharpen his claws on your Art Deco dressing table? Yes, you're guilty and your sins will out.**

that marijuana may never be either legal or widely available again, but if you're feeling morose, do your cat a favor. Let him stay with the fun couple down the hall. Call him later when you feel better.

While we're on the subject of guilt, who takes care of your cat when you're out of town? Do you just leave her alone in the apartment, with some water and dry food? Do you board her where she can pick up diseases or bad politics...or do you ask the old guy down the block to look in on her occasionally while you're gone? How well do you know this guy? Did you ask for references? Remember that movie *The Hand That Rocks the Cradle* with Rebecca De Mornay? Always check their references, because if you cause your cat distress in this world, you may pay for it in the next.

thanks...

Design for "Cat Bathroom and Solarium" by Debra McQueen, architect.

Lyrics for "Pussy Cats in Heaven" written by Nicole Hollander, Tom Mula, Arnold Aprill, and Steve Rashid.

Grateful acknowledgment to Mr. Paul Kunkel for the helpful advice contained in his book *How to Toilet Train Your Cat*.

*Nicole Hollander with the late John Hollander, playing his favorite game: Kidnapped.*

Nicole Hollander is the author of the syndicated cartoon strip "Sylvia," which appears in eighty papers nationwide, including the *Chicago Tribune*, the *Boston Globe*, and the *L.A. Times*.

Nicole lives in Chicago and shares her flat with two lovely guys, Buddy and Izzy. The cats like leaping from high places onto unsuspecting visitors. All three enjoy reading aloud and making elaborate plans for trips they never take.

*My Cat's Not Fat, He's Just Big Boned* is another cartoon collection from "Sylvia" cartoonist Nicole Hollander. Featuring cats who hypnotize their owners, cats who plot dastardly deeds but get distracted, and of course cats obsessed with food, food, food. This hilarious compilation is just right for kitty-lovers everywhere.

**ISBN-10: 1-4022-0861-8**
**ISBN-13: 978-1-4022-0861-4**

Hysteria books are available at book and gift stores everywhere.

*Psycho Kitties* is a cartoon collection from Nicole Hollander. Featuring cats who won't let you leave the house, cats who won't let you date, cats who are worse than bad . . . if you're dealing with a deranged kitty, know that you are not alone!

ISBN-10: 1-4022-0729-8
ISBN-13: 978-1-4022-0729-7

Hysteria books are available at book and gift stores everywhere.